Grounded and Free

A Practical Guide to Sobriety and Building a Life You Can Stay In

By

M. Nickleson Battle, Jr.,
Ed. D, LPC, CCTP, CCAPT, BC-TMH

&

Latonia Laffitte,
Ed D, LPC, NCC, BC-TMH.

Genre: Non-fiction, faith/religion, mental health, meditation, journaling, affirmations, self-help

Disclaimer

This workbook is intended for educational and supportive purposes only and is not a substitute for professional medical or mental health treatment. Individuals are encouraged to seek guidance from licensed professionals as needed.

Published by: Nick of Time Publishing

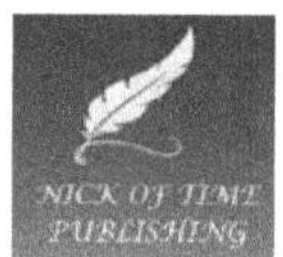

This workbook is intended for educational and supportive purposes only. It is not
intended to replace professional medical, psychological, or psychiatric care. Individuals
are encouraged to seek guidance from licensed healthcare providers as needed.

The content within this publication is based on established psychological principles,
clinical experience, and trauma-informed care practices. Any references to diagnostic
criteria are aligned with generally accepted standards, including those outlined in the
DSM-5-TR.

Authors: M. Nickleson Battle, Jr., Ed. D, LPC, CCTP, CCAPT, BC-TMH, and
Latonia Laffitte, Ed. D, NCC, LCP, BC-TMH

Table of Contents

Introduction:
This Book Is for You

If you are holding this book, there is a reason.

Maybe you're tired.

Tired of starting over.

Tired of feeling like you know what to do but still ending up in the same place.

Tired of feeling unstable, overwhelmed, or stuck.

Or maybe you're at the beginning.

Trying to understand what a new life even means.

Trying to figure out where to start.

Trying to believe that something different is possible.

Wherever you are, this book is for you.

This Is Not a Book You Just Read

This is a book you use.

You don't need to:

- Understand everything at once
- Do every exercise perfectly
- Have it all figured out

You just need to:

- Show up
- Be honest
- Try

Some days you'll read a few pages.

Some days you'll come back to the same section again and again.

Some days you won't want to open it at all.

That's part of the process.

Sobriety Is Not About Perfection

Let's get this clear from the beginning:

A new life is not about:

- Being perfect
- Never struggling
- Getting everything right

A new life is about:

- Learning how to respond differently
- Catching yourself earlier
- Building stability over time

It's about progress.

Not perfection.

You Are Not Starting from Zero

Even if it feels like it.

You've already:

- Survived difficult things
- Found ways to cope (even if they weren't sustainable)
- Kept going when it would have been easier to stop

This book is not here to tear you down.

It's here to help you **build something stronger**.

This Book Is Built Around Real Life

This is not written like a textbook.

You won't find:

- Complicated language
- Clinical explanations you can't use
- Abstract ideas that don't apply to your life

Instead, you'll find:

- What's actually happening inside you
- Why you respond the way you do
- What you can do differently right now

You Don't Have to Do This Alone, But You Do Have to Do the Work

This book is a tool.

It supports:

- **Therapy** • **Group work** • **Your new life**

But it also stands on its own.

Because there will be moments when:

- No one is around
- You feel overwhelmed
- You have to make a decision

And in those moments, you need something you can turn to.

A Word About Strength

Strength is not:

- Pushing everything down
- Pretending you're fine
- Handling everything alone

Real strength is:

- Being honest about where you are
- Facing what's difficult
- Choosing differently even when it's uncomfortable

Culture, Community, and Healing

Healing does not happen in isolation.

For many of us, strength has often meant:

- Carrying more than we should
- Holding things in
- Surviving without support

But survival and healing are not the same thing.

You deserve more than survival.

You deserve:

- Love
- Peace
- Connection
- Stability
- Joy
- A life that feels like it can hold you

This book will talk about **your village,** because who you have around you matters.

Not just anybody.

The right people.

How to Use This Book

Each chapter will include:

- Clear explanations
- Practical tools
- Reflection exercises
- Worksheets you can actually use

You don't need to do everything at once.

Start where you are.

Come back when you need to.

Final Thought Before We Begin

You are not broken.

You are someone who has learned certain ways of coping.

Some of those ways worked for a while.

Now it's time to build something that works **long-term**.

A Foundation for Your New Life: The Grounded Alignment Framework™

Before you move forward, you need a foundation.

Not just information.

Not just ideas.

You need a way to think, respond, and move through your new life consistently and intentionally.

That is what this framework provides.

Introducing the Grounded Alignment Framework™

The Grounded Alignment Framework™ is a practical system to help you stay aware, make intentional decisions, and stay aligned with the life you are building.

You will use this throughout this workbook.

Especially when:

- You feel overwhelmed
- You feel triggered
- You feel unsure of what to do next
- You feel pulled back toward old habits

This Is Not Something You Memorize

This is something you use.

The 5 Pillars of the Grounded Alignment Framework™

1. Awareness
2. Ownership
3. Alignment
4. Connection
5. Purpose

These five areas help you stay:

- Grounded
- Stable
- Focused
- Intentional

Awareness — Seeing Clearly

You cannot change what you do not recognize.

Awareness means:

- Knowing what you feel
- Recognizing your thoughts
- Understanding your patterns

"What is really happening right now?"

Ownership — Taking Responsibility

This is where your power comes from.

Ownership means:

- Taking responsibility for your choices
- Recognizing that your decisions shape your outcomes

"What part of this is mine—and what am I going to do about it?"

Alignment: Living in Integrity

Alignment means your actions match:

- Your values
- Your goals
- The life you are building

"Does this move me forward or backward?"

Connection — You Are Not Alone

Your new life requires connection.

Connection means:

- Staying engaged with your village
- Reaching out when needed
- Allowing support

"Who is helping me stay on track?"

Purpose — Why You Keep Going

You need more than avoiding relapse.

You need a reason to stay.

Purpose can be:

- Stability
- Growth
- Peace
- Showing up for yourself

"What am I building—and why does it matter?"

How to Use This Framework

When you feel:

- Triggered
- Overwhelmed
- Stuck

Pause and walk through this:

- What am I feeling? (*Awareness*)
- What do I need to take responsibility for? (*Ownership*)
- What choice aligns with my growth? (*Alignment*)
- Who can I connect with? (*Connection*)
- What am I working toward? (*Purpose*)

Spiritual Component: Staying Grounded in Who You Are Becoming

This framework is also spiritual.

Not religious.

It is about:

- Being intentional
- Being aware
- Being aligned
- Staying connected
- Living with purpose

You are not who you used to be.

You are becoming someone new.

This framework helps you stay grounded in that process.

CLOSING THOUGHT

You don't need to have everything figured out.

You just need something to return to.

This is your foundation.

And throughout this workbook:

You will continue coming back to it.

Awareness — Seeing Clearly

Your new life begins with honesty and understanding. In this pillar, you will look at your patterns, your pain, and the ways your mind and body have learned to respond..

01 Why Change Is So Hard

If change were easy, you would have already done it.

That's not a judgment.

That's the truth.

You're Not Fighting Just One Thing

When you try to change, you're not just fighting:

- A habit
- A substance
- A behavior

You're also fighting:

- Patterns your brain has learned
- Emotional responses that happen automatically
- Ways of coping that feel familiar

The Habit Loop (Real Life Version)

Every behavior you repeat follows a pattern.

It looks like this:

Trigger → **Thought** → **Feeling** → **Action** → **Result**

Let's slow that down.

Trigger

Something happens.

- You feel stressed
- Someone says something
- You feel alone
- You get overwhelmed

Thought

Your mind reacts quickly.

- "I can't deal with this."
- "I need something to calm down."
- "This is too much."

Feeling

Your body responds.

- Anxiety
- Anger
- Sadness
- Restlessness

Action

You do what you've learned works.

- Use
- Avoid
- Shut down
- React

Result

You get relief.

But only temporarily.

Why Your Brain Keeps Going Back

Your brain is not trying to ruin your life.

It's trying to:

Solve problems as quickly as possible.

If something worked before, even temporarily, your brain remembers.

And it goes back to it.

This Is Why You Feel Stuck

Because even when you *know* something isn't good for you...

It still feels like:

- The easiest option
- The fastest relief
- The most familiar response

Change Feels Uncomfortable on Purpose

When you try something new, it feels:

- Awkward
- Slow
- Unnatural

That's because it's not wired yet.

Old patterns feel automatic.

New patterns feel forced.

At first.

The Goal Is Not to "Stop Everything"

The goal is to:

Catch the pattern earlier.

You don't have to get it perfect.

You just need to start noticing:

- What triggers you
- What you tell yourself
- What you do next

Example (Real Life)

Trigger: You feel overwhelmed after a long day

Thought: "I need something to calm down"

Feeling: Anxiety

Action: Use

New Pattern:

Trigger: Same

Thought: "This is a lot right now"

Feeling: Anxiety

Action: Pause, breathe, step away

It doesn't feel as strong at first.

But it builds.

What You're Really Doing

You're not just stopping something.

You're:

- Rewiring your responses
- Teaching your brain a new way
- Building something that lasts

Worksheet: My Pattern (Take Your Time)

Think about a recent situation.

Write it out honestly.

1. What happened (trigger):

____

____

____

2. What did I think in that moment:

____

____

____

3. What did I feel (emotion/body):

____

____

____

4. What did I do (action):

____

____

____

5. What happened after (result):

____

____

____

Now Try This

What could I do differently next time (even a small change):

____

____

____

Journaling Page

- What patterns do I notice?

- What shows up again and again?

CLOSING THOUGHT

You are not stuck.

You are patterned.

And patterns can change.

Why You Used and What It Was Doing for You

Before you can change something, you have to understand it.

Not just on the surface.
Not just "I use because it's a habit" or "I use because I messed up."

You have to understand:

What it was doing for you.

Because if you don't understand that, you'll keep trying to remove something without replacing what it gave you.

And that's where people get stuck.

Let's Be Honest About This

Substance use is not random.

At some point, it made sense.

It helped.

It worked.

Maybe not long-term—but in the moment, it did something for you.

Common Reasons People Use

You might see yourself in one or more of these.

1. To Calm Down

When your mind won't slow down

When your body feels tense

When anxiety is high

Substances can feel like:

- Relief
- Quiet
- Control

2. To Escape

When things feel overwhelming

When emotions feel too heavy

When you don't want to think about something

Using becomes a way to:

- Not feel
- Not think
- Not deal

3. To Feel Something

Sometimes it's not about too much feeling.

It's about not feeling anything at all.

- Numbness
- Emptiness
- Disconnection

Substances can temporarily bring:

- Emotion
- Energy
- A sense of being alive

4. **To Slow Your Mind (ADHD, Anxiety, Overthinking)**

If your mind is always moving:

- Jumping from thought to thought
- Unable to focus
- Constantly restless

Substances may feel like:

- A way to slow down   •   A way to focus   •   A way to settle

5. **To Feel Confident or Connected**

In social situations:

- Feeling anxious
- Feeling like you don't fit
- Feeling guarded

Substances can make you feel:

- More open •   More confident   •   More connected

The Problem Isn't Just the Behavior

The problem is:

The behavior became your solution.

So when you try to remove it...

Your brain asks:

"What am I supposed to do instead?"

Why It Stops Working

Over time, things change.

What once helped begins to hurt.

You may notice:

- You need more to get the same effect
- The relief doesn't last as long
- The consequences get worse
- Your problems increase

Now you're in a cycle:

You need it   →   but it's also hurting you

The Trap

You're not just dealing with substance use.

You're dealing with:

- Emotional pain
- Stress
- Thoughts
- Patterns

And the substance is still the fastest way your brain knows how to respond.

This Is Not About Blame

This is important.

Understanding why you use is not about:

- Justifying it
- Excusing it

It's about:

Getting clear on what needs to be replaced.

You Can't Just Remove Something You Have to Replace It

This is one of the biggest mistakes people make.

They focus on:

"I just need to stop."

But stopping alone doesn't work in the long term.

Because when you remove something that was helping you cope, even if it was unhealthy, you create a gap.

And your brain does not like gaps.

What Happens When You Don't Replace It

If you take something away and don't replace it, you will feel:

- Restless
- Uncomfortable
- Irritated
- Empty
- Overwhelmed

And your brain will start searching for something to fill that space.

That's when people:

- Go back to using
- Replace it with another unhealthy behavior
- Feel like they're "failing."

But what's really happening is:

Nothing replaced what was removed.

Think About It Like This

Substance use wasn't just a problem.

It was also functioning as:

- Stress relief
- Emotional control
- Escape
- Stimulation
- Connection

So when you remove it, you're not just removing a behavior.

You're removing a **tool your brain was using**.

You Still Need Something in That Place

Your new life is not just about stopping.

It is about building.

You are replacing:

• Short-term relief	→	with real regulation
• Avoidance	→	with coping
• Chaos	→	with structure
• Disconnection	→	with real connection

Real Example

Let's break this down clearly.

Old Pattern

You feel overwhelmed

→ You use

→ You feel relief

If You Just Stop

You feel overwhelmed

→ You have nothing to do

→ You feel worse

→ You go back

New Pattern (What You're Building)

You feel overwhelmed

→ You pause

→ You use a skill (breathing, stepping away, calling someone)

→ You get relief (maybe slower—but real)

Replacement Feels Weaker at First

This is important.

New coping skills:

- Feel slower
- Feel less intense
- Don't give immediate relief the same way

That doesn't mean they don't work.

It means:

They haven't been practiced yet.

You Are Building Strength, Not Just Relief

Substances give quick relief.

Skills build long-term strength.

Ask Yourself This

Every time you feel the urge, ask:

"What do I actually need right now?"

Not:

- "How do I stop this feeling?"

But:

- "What is this feeling asking for?"

Examples of Replacement

If you used to:

Calm anxiety → try:

- Breathing
- Walking
- Sitting still and grounding

Escape stress → try:

- Stepping away
- Writing it out
- Talking to someone

Feel something → try:

- Music
- Movement
- Being around people

- Deep breathing
- Structure
- Focused tasks

This Is the Shift

You are moving from:

"Take something away"

to:

"Build something better"

Worksheet: Why I Use (Be Honest with Yourself)

1. What do I feel right before I use?

____

____

____

____

2. What am I usually thinking in that moment?

____

____

____

____

3. What does using do for me in the moment?
(Be specific—what does it help with?)

____

____

____

____

4. What happens after?
   (Short-term vs long-term)

____

____

____

____

5. What problem was I trying to solve?

____

____

____

____

Worksheet: Replacement Plan

What I usually use for:

____

____

____

____

What I actually need in those moments:

____

____

____

____

One thing I can try instead:

____

____

____

____

What I expect it to feel like at first:

____

____

____

____

Reminder to myself:
"Just because it feels different doesn't mean it doesn't work."

Journaling Page

- What patterns am I starting to notice?

- What shows up the most for me?

CLOSING THOUGHT

ou didn't just develop a habit.

You developed a system for coping.

Now you're building a better one.

03 Trauma, Why Your Body Reacts the Way It Does

There are moments when your reaction feels bigger than the situation.

Someone says something small, and you feel angry fast.

Something reminds you of the past, and your body tightens up.

You shut down, pull away, or feel like you're not fully there.

And sometimes you think:

"Why am I reacting like this?"

This Is Not Random

Your reactions are not random.

They are learned.

They are stored.

And most importantly:

They are your body trying to protect you.

What Trauma Actually Is

Let's define this clearly.

Trauma is not just about what happened.

Trauma is about your mental, physical, emotional, and even spiritual response to what happened.

Two people can experience the same situation and be affected very differently.

Because trauma is not just the event.

It's:

- How your body responded
- How your mind processed it
- What it meant to you
- What stayed with you afterward

Clinical Definition

From a clinical standpoint, the DSM-5 (and DSM-5-TR) defines trauma as:

Exposure to actual or threatened death, serious injury, or sexual violence.

This exposure can happen in different ways:

- Directly experiencing it
- Witnessing it happen to others
- Learning that it happened to someone close to you
- Being repeatedly exposed to it (for example, through work or environment)

Important Clarification

You do not have to respond in a certain way for something to "count" as trauma.

It does **not require** that you felt:

- Intense fear
- Helplessness
- Horror

in the moment for it to qualify.

Trauma Is Not Limited to Direct Experience

You do not have to experience something directly for it to impact you.

You can be affected by something you:

- Witnessed
- Heard about
- Learned about
- Were exposed to over time
- Grew up around

Your system still reacts.

Your body still processes it.

And it can still shape how you respond today.

Your Body Remembers

Even when you don't think about it.

Even when you try to move on.

Your body keeps track of:

- Stress
- Fear
- Pain
- Threat

So when something feels similar, even slightly, your system reacts.

The Three Main Trauma Responses

Your body has built-in survival responses.

They are automatic.

They are fast.

And they don't always match what's actually happening now.

1. Fight (Overreacting / Pushing Back)

You may:

- Get angry quickly
- Feel irritated or defensive
- Want to argue or control the situation

Your system is saying:
"Protect yourself."

2. Flight (Avoiding / Escaping)

You may:

- Avoid people or situations
- Feel anxious or restless
- Want to leave or get away

Your system is saying:
"Get out."

3. Freeze / Shutdown (Numb / Disconnected)

You may:

- Feel numb
- Feel stuck
- Shut down emotionally
- Disconnect from what's happening

Your system is saying:
"Don't feel. Stay still."

Why This Matters

If you don't understand your trauma responses:

- You think something is wrong with you
- You react without knowing why
- You try to escape the feeling

And that's where substance use often comes in.

Trauma and Substance Use Are Connected

Substances often become a way to:

- Calm your system down
- Escape overwhelming feelings
- Feel something when you're numb
- Avoid triggers

At some point, it worked.

That's why your brain keeps going back to it.

The Problem Now

The same thing that helped before...

Is now hurting you.

And your system hasn't learned a new way yet.

You Are Not "Too Sensitive"

You are not:

- Weak
- Broken
- Overreacting

You are responding based on what your system learned.

Your Body Is Trying to Keep You Safe

Even if the situation is not dangerous now.

Your body doesn't always know the difference between:

- Then
- And now

The Goal Is Not to "Turn It Off"

You cannot force trauma responses away.

Trying to ignore them usually makes them stronger.

The goal is:

To learn how to bring yourself back.

Coming Back to the Present

When you are triggered, your system shifts into the past.

Building your new life means learning how to say:

"That was then. This is now."

Grounding: Bringing Yourself Back

Grounding is how you reconnect to the present moment.

Not just in your thoughts.

In your body.

Simple Grounding Practice

Look around and say (out loud or in your head):

- Where am I?
- What day is it?
- What is actually happening right now?

Then:

- Put your feet flat on the ground
- Press your hands together
- Take a slow breath

Short Statement to Use

When you feel triggered, say:

"I am here. I am safe right now."

Even if you don't fully believe it yet.

Say it anyway.

Body-Based Reset

Your body needs signals of safety.

Try:

- Splashing cold water on your face
- Holding something cold
- Taking slow, deep breaths
- Sitting still and feeling your body

Why This Works

Because trauma lives in the body.

So healing has to involve the body.

You Don't Have to Figure Everything Out Right Now

You don't need to:

- Understand every memory
- Process everything at once
- Fix everything immediately

You just need to:

Learn how to stay present when your system reacts.

Real-Life Example

Situation

Someone raises their voice.

Your Reaction

Your body tenses.

Your heart races.

You feel angry or shut down.

What's Actually Happening

Your system is reacting based on past experiences—whether you lived them, witnessed them, or were exposed to them over time.

New Response

Pause

Breathe

Ground yourself

Remind yourself:

"This is not the same situation."

This Is Practice

Not perfection.

At first, you will:

- React quickly
- Realize it later
- Try again next time

Over time:

- You catch it sooner
- You respond differently
- You feel more in control

Worksheet:
My Trauma Responses

When I feel overwhelmed, I usually:

- ☐ Get angry
- ☐ Shut down
- ☐ Avoid
- ☐ Feel anxious
- ☐ Feel numb

Situations that trigger me:

____

____

____

____

What my body feels like when I'm triggered:

____

____

____

____

What I usually do in those moments:

Worksheet: Grounding Plan

When I feel triggered, I will:

1. _______________________________________

2. _______________________________________

3. _______________________________________

A phrase I will use:

____

____

____

____

Something physical I can do to calm down:

____

____

____

____

Journaling Page

- What have I experienced, witnessed, or been exposed to that may still affect me today?

- What patterns do I see in how I react?

- What helps me feel even a little safer?

CLOSING THOUGHT

Your reactions make sense.

Even if they don't help you anymore.

You're not trying to erase your past.

You're learning how to live in the present.

Pillar II

Ownership — Taking Responsibility

Ownership is where change becomes real. In this pillar, you will examine your mental health, your internal narrative, and your responsibility for how you respond.

04 Understanding Your Mental Health, Real Life, Not Labels

Let's Address the Elephant in the Room

Before we go any further, we need to talk about something directly.

A lot of people use substances not just to "get high" or "escape."

They use because they are trying to manage something deeper.

Many people are self-medicating mental health symptoms.

That means:

- Trying to calm anxiety
- Trying to stabilize mood
- Trying to slow down racing thoughts
- Trying to feel something instead of nothing

And for a while, it can feel like it works.

Self-Medication Is Common—But It Comes at a Cost

At some point, the substance becomes:

- The way you cope
- The way you regulate
- The way you function

But over-time:

- It stops working the same way

- It creates new problems
- It makes the original issues worse

Understanding Co-Occurring Disorders (Comorbidity)

There's a term for when substance use and mental health conditions happen together:

Co-occurring disorders (also called comorbidity).

This is not rare.

It's common.

Many people are dealing with both:

- Substance use
- Mental health challenges

At the same time.

Why This Matters

If you only focus on stopping substance use, but ignore mental health:

- The symptoms are still there
- The discomfort is still there
- The need for relief is still there

And that increases the risk of going back.

Let's Talk About Stigma (Be Honest About This)

In many communities, especially in African American communities, mental health has not always been openly talked about.

You may have heard things like:

- "Just be strong"
- "Pray on it"

- "You'll be alright"
- "Don't claim that"

At the same time...

Substance use may be:

- More normalized
- More accepted socially
- Less talked about as a "problem"

Let's Be Real About What "Normalized" Means

When we talk about substance use being normalized, we have to be honest about where it often starts.

Alcohol and cigarettes are substances.

They are widely accepted.

They are legal.

They are often introduced early:

- At family gatherings
- Social events
- Celebrations
- Stressful situations

Because they are socially accepted, they often don't get seen as "the problem."

The Gateway Reality

For many people, alcohol and cigarettes become the **starting point**.

They can:

- Lower your guard
- Introduce the idea of using something to cope
- Become a regular habit

And over time, they can open the door to:

- Increased use
- Stronger substances
- Dependence

Why This Matters

If something is normalized, you may not question it.

You may think:

- "It's just a drink"
- "Everybody does it"
- "This isn't the real issue"

But for many people:

This is where the pattern begins.

The Reality

It may feel more acceptable to say:

- "I just need something to take the edge off"

Than to say:

- "I'm dealing with anxiety, depression, or bipolar symptoms"

But one leads to long-term healing.

The other keeps you stuck.

This Is Not About Judgment

This is about awareness.

Because once you understand what's really happening:

You can start addressing the right problem.

You Are Not Your Diagnosis

Let's be clear:

A diagnosis is not your identity.

It is:

- A way to understand patterns
- A way to guide treatment
- A way to find the right support

Why Getting the Right Help Matters

If you are dealing with mental health symptoms:

- Therapy matters
- Structure matters
- Support matters

And for many people:

Medication can be an important part of stability.

Medication Compliance (Let's Be Direct)

This is where people struggle.

You may:

- Stop taking medication when you feel better
- Not like how it makes you feel
- Feel like you don't need it

But inconsistency leads to:

- Mood instability
- Increased symptoms
- Higher relapse risk

Key Truth

Stability supports sobriety.

And for many people:

Medication is part of that stability.

This Is About Balance, Not Dependence

Medication is not:

- A weakness
- A failure
- A replacement for growth

It is:

- A support
- A tool
- A way to help your system regulate

Real-Life Understanding of Mental Health Conditions

Bipolar Disorder (Plain Language with DSM-Based Understanding)

Clinically, bipolar disorder involves:

Periods of elevated mood (mania or hypomania) and periods of depression.

What That Looks Like in Real Life

Elevated periods may include:	Depressive periods may include:
- Less need for sleep	- Low energy
- Increased energy	- Loss of interest
- Racing thoughts	- Feeling heavy or stuck

- Impulsivity
- Negative thinking
- Feeling unusually confident
- Isolation

Major Depression

Clinically, depression involves:

Persistent low mood or loss of interest, along with changes in energy, sleep, thinking, and motivation.

Real-Life Experience

- Everything feels harder
- Motivation is low
- Even small tasks feel overwhelming
- You may feel disconnected or hopeless

ADHD (Attention-Deficit/Hyperactivity Disorder)

Clinically, ADHD involves:

Ongoing patterns of inattention and/or impulsivity that affect functioning.

Real-Life Experience

- Difficulty focusing
- Starting things but not finishing
- Feeling restless
- Acting without thinking
- Struggling with consistency

Anxiety Disorders

Clinically, anxiety involves:

Excessive worry, fear, or nervous system activation that is difficult to control.

Real-Life Experience

- Racing thoughts
- Constant worry
- Physical tension
- Feeling on edge
- Difficulty relaxing

Schizoaffective Disorder (Plain Language)

Clinically, this involves:

A combination of mood symptoms (like depression or bipolar) along with disturbances in thinking or perception.

Real-Life Experience

- Mood changes
- Confusion in thinking
- Difficulty distinguishing what's real vs. what feels real
- Periods of disconnection

Bringing It All Together

You may relate to one of these.

You may relate to several.

That does not mean something is "wrong" with you.

It means:

You have patterns that need the right kind of support.

The Real Goal

Not:

- "Fix everything overnight"

But:

Understand what you're dealing with—and respond differently.

Worksheet:
My Mental Health Patterns

What I struggle with most:

____

____

____

What it feels like day-to-day:

____

____

____

What helps me feel more stable:

____

____

____

What I may need support with:

____

____

____

Worksheet:
My Treatment Plan Awareness

Am I currently receiving support (therapy, medication, etc.)?

____

____

____

If not, what is one step I can take?

____

____

____

If I am on medication, am I taking it consistently?

____

____

____

What gets in the way of consistency?

____

____

____

Journaling Page

- What have I been trying to manage on my own?

- What patterns started small but became bigger over time?

CLOSING THOUGHT

You are not weak for needing help.

You are not broken for having symptoms.

You are someone learning how to manage your mind, your body, and your life in a healthier way.

05 Thoughts, Beliefs, and the Story You Tell Yourself

There is something happening inside you all the time.

Even when you're quiet.

Even when nothing is going on around you.

There is a voice.

A running conversation.

A way you interpret:

- What happens
- What people say
- What you feel
- Who you think you are

That Voice Matters More Than You Think

Because it shapes:

- How you feel
- What you believe
- What you do next

This Is the Part Most People Don't Notice

You don't just react to situations.

You react to the meaning you give them.

Example

Someone doesn't respond to your message.

Possible Thought #1

"They're ignoring me."

→ Feeling: Hurt

→ Reaction: Pull away or get upset

Possible Thought #2

"They might be busy."

→ Feeling: Neutral

→ Reaction: Wait

Same situation.

Different thought.

Different outcome.

Your Thoughts Become Your Reality

Not because they are always true.

But because they feel true.

Where Do These Thoughts Come From?

They don't come out of nowhere.

They are shaped by:

- Past experiences
- Trauma
- Relationships
- What you were taught
- What you've been through

Over Time, Thoughts Become Beliefs

A thought repeated enough becomes something deeper.

It becomes:

A belief.

Common Core Beliefs

You may not say them out loud, but they show up in how you think:

- "I'm not enough."
- "People always leave."
- "I can't trust anyone."
- "I'll never get it right."
- "I'm too much" or "not enough."

From Beliefs to Narratives

This is where it goes even deeper.

When beliefs repeat over time, they don't just stay as thoughts.

They turn into a **narrative**.

What Is a Narrative?

A narrative is:

The story you tell yourself about who you are and how your life works.

It's not just one thought.

It's a pattern of thoughts that create a storyline.

Examples of Narratives

- "I always mess things up."
- "People don't stay."

- "Nothing ever works out for me."
- "I have to handle everything on my own."
- "I can't trust anyone."

Why Narratives Matter

Because once a narrative forms, you start to:

- Look for evidence that supports it
- Ignore evidence that doesn't
- Act in ways that keep it going

Example of a Narrative in Action

Narrative:

"People always leave me."

What happens next:

- You expect people to leave
- You become guarded or reactive
- The relationship becomes strained
- The person pulls away

Now it feels like proof.

But the narrative helped shape the outcome.

Narratives and Substance Use

Narratives play a big role.

If your narrative is:

"I can't handle life without something"

Then your behavior will follow that.

If your narrative becomes:

"I'm learning how to handle things differently"

That opens the door for change.

This Is Not About Blaming Yourself

You didn't create these narratives on purpose.

They developed over time.

From:

- What you experienced
- What you were told
- What you went through

But You Can Start Changing Them

Not overnight.

Not all at once.

But one piece at a time.

The Spiritual Layer: Meaning, Identity, and Inner Direction

There is another level to this work.

Not just what you think.

Not just what you believe.

But:

What you believe your life means.

Spiritual Does Not Mean Religious

Spirituality is not about:

- **Religion**   • **Rules**   • **Beliefs you have to follow**

Spirituality is about:

- **Meaning**   • **Purpose**
- **Connection**   • **Direction**

Why This Matters

Without meaning, you can feel like:

- Just stopping something
- Just getting through the day
- Just trying not to go back

That's not enough in the long-term.

You need something that makes you want to stay.

The Deeper Question

Not just:

"How do I stop using?"

But:

"What am I building instead?"

Your Inner Narrative and Your Direction

Your narrative doesn't just affect your behavior.

It affects your direction.

If your story is:

"Nothing works out for me"

Then your life will start to reflect that.

If your story becomes:

"I'm building something different, even if it's slow"

Your direction changes.

Connection to Self

Part of healing is reconnecting with yourself.

Not the version shaped by:

- Pain
- Trauma
- Survival

But the version of you that is:

- Aware
- Intentional
- Capable of growth

Connection to Something Greater

This does not have to be defined.

But many people find strength in connecting to:

- Purpose
- Values
- Something beyond immediate struggle

Questions to Consider

- What keeps me going?
- What matters to me?

- What kind of life do I want to build?

Meaning Helps You Stay

When things get hard—and they will—

Skills help.

But meaning keeps you going.

Your Voice Matters Most

As you begin to understand your thoughts, beliefs, and narratives, there is something important you need to recognize.

There are a lot of voices around you.

- People's opinions
- Past criticism
- Expectations
- What you were told growing up
- What others think you should be

All of that can get loud.

And if you're not careful, those voices can start to shape how you see yourself.

But Here Is the Truth

Of all the voices in the crowd, yours has to be the loudest.

Because your voice is the one that stays with you.

Your voice is the one you wake up with.

Your voice is the one you carry throughout the day.

Your voice is the one that shows up when things get hard.

You Have to Be Your Loudest Support

That doesn't mean ignoring reality.

It means learning how to support yourself in a real way.

Not tearing yourself down.

Not reinforcing old narratives.

But saying:

- "This is hard, but I'm still here."
- "I've made mistakes, but I'm still moving forward."
- "I'm learning how to do this differently."

What You Say to Yourself Matters

If your inner voice is:

- Critical
- Harsh
- Defeating

Then even small challenges feel overwhelming.

But if your inner voice becomes:

- Steady
- Honest
- Supportive

Then you build resilience.

What You Know About Yourself Matters More

There will be people who:

- Misunderstand you
- Judge you

- Doubt you
- Define you based on your past

But:

What you know about yourself matters more than what anyone else thinks about you.

Because they don't:

- Live in your mind
- Feel what you feel
- Know your effort
- See your internal growth

This Is Part of Rewriting Your Narrative

Old narrative:

"I'm not enough."

"People define who I am."

New narrative:

"I know who I am becoming."

"My voice matters."

"I can support myself through this."

This Is Not About Ego It's About Grounding

Being your loudest voice is not about:

- Arrogance
- Ignoring feedback
- Acting like you don't need anyone

It's about:

Staying grounded in yourself while you grow.

You Rewrite the Story Through Action

This is key.

You don't just think differently.

You act differently.

And over time:

Your actions begin to rewrite your narrative—and your sense of meaning.

Real-Life Shift

Old Thought

"I can't handle this."

Old Narrative

"I'm not capable."

New Thought

"This is hard, but I can get through it."

New Narrative

"I'm learning how to handle things, even when it's difficult."

Deeper Meaning

"I'm becoming someone stronger and more stable."

This Is the Work

Not just stopping behavior.

But changing:

- Thoughts
- Beliefs
- Narratives
- **And the meaning you attach to your life**

Skill: Catch It, Check It, Change It

1. Catch It

Notice the thought.

"What am I telling myself right now?"

2. Check It

Ask:

- Is this true?
- Is this helpful?
- Is this part of an old story?

3. Change It

Replace it with something more accurate.

Worksheet: Catch It, Check It, Change It

Situation:

____

____

____

____

What I thought:

____

____

____

____

What I felt:

____

____

____

____

Is this thought 100% true?

Is this part of an old narrative? If so, which one?

A more balanced thought:

Worksheet: My Core Beliefs

A belief I have about myself:

____

____

____

Where this belief may have come from:

____

____

____

How it affects me:

____

____

____

A new belief I want to start building:

____

____

____

Worksheet: My Narrative

The story I often tell myself about my life:

____

____

____

Where this story may have come from:

____

____

____

How this story has affected my choices:

____

____

____

A new story I want to begin building:

____

____

____

Worksheet:
Meaning and Direction

What gives my life meaning right now (even a little):

____

____

____

What matters most to me:

____

____

____

The kind of life I want to build:

____

____

____

One step I can take in that direction:

____

____

____

Journaling Page

- What story have I been living by?

- Does that story help me or hold me back?

- What kind of life do I actually want to build?

CLOSING THOUGHT

You are not your thoughts.

You are not your past.

And you are not stuck in one story.

You are someone who can rewrite it and build a life that reflects who you are becoming.

What To Do When You're Triggered? Real-Time Skills

There are moments when everything happens fast.

Something is said.

Something happens.

Something shifts inside you.

And before you even realize it...

You're reacting.

What a Trigger Actually Is

A trigger is:

Anything that activates an emotional, mental, or physical response.

It can be:

- Something someone says
- A memory
- A situation
- A feeling
- Even a thought

Triggers Are Not the Problem

This is important.

Triggers are not the problem.

Your response to the trigger is what matters.

Why Triggers Feel So Strong

When you are triggered:

- Your body reacts quickly
- Your thoughts speed up
- Your emotions intensify

This is not random.

This is your system doing what it has learned to do.

The Pattern (Fast Version)

Trigger → **Thought** → **Feeling** → **Result**

And most of the time, this happens automatically.

The Goal

You are not trying to:

- Eliminate triggers
- Control everything around you

You are learning how to:

Respond instead of react.

Step One: Slow It Down

When you're triggered, everything speeds up.

Your job is to slow it down—even a little.

Pause (Even for a Few Seconds)

You don't have to get it perfect.

Just create space.

Simple Pause Statement

Say to yourself:

"Pause. Something just got activated."

That alone begins to shift your response.

Step Two: Name What's Happening

When you name it, you gain some control over it.

Ask Yourself

- What just happened?
- What am I feeling?
- What is my body doing right now?

Example

"I feel tight. My chest is heavy. I'm getting irritated."

This brings you out of automatic reaction.

Step Three: Ground Your Body

You cannot think your way out of a trigger.

You have to bring your body down first.

Grounding Techniques

- Put your feet flat on the ground
- Press your hands together
- Take slow, deep breaths
- Look around and name 3 things you see

Short Statement

"I'm here. I'm safe right now."

Even if it doesn't feel fully true yet.

Step Four: Choose Your Response

This is where change happens.

Not in the trigger.

But in what you do next.

Ask Yourself

"What is the next right step?"

Not:

- "How do I fix everything?"

Just:

- "What's one better response right now?"

Options May Include

- Walking away
- Taking a break
- Calling someone
- Staying quiet instead of reacting
- Using a skill

This Is Where Most People Struggle

Because the old response feels automatic.

And the new response feels:

- Slower
- Weaker
- Less satisfying at first

But This Is the Shift

You are moving from:

Reaction $\rightarrow$ **to** $\rightarrow$ **Response**

Understanding Emotional Intensity

When you are triggered, your emotions can feel:

- Strong
- Overwhelming
- Urgent

Important Truth

Just because something feels urgent does not mean you have to act on it.

Emotions Rise and Fall

They don't stay at the same level forever.

If you don't react immediately, they often:

- Peak
- Then decrease

The Urge Will Pass

This is especially important for substance use.

When You Feel the Urge

It may feel like:

- "I need something right now."
- "I can't deal with this."

But Urges Work Like Waves	Your Job Is to Ride It Out
They rise	Not fight it.
They peak	Not act on it.
They pass	Just get through it.

Real-Life Example

Situation

Someone says something that feels disrespectful.

Old Pattern

Thought: "They're disrespecting me."
Feeling: Anger
Action: React immediately

New Pattern

Pause
Notice
Ground
Respond with intention

Even if it's just:

- Saying less
- Walking away
- Giving yourself space

Your Voice Matters in This Moment Too

When you are triggered, other voices can get loud:

- "React now"
- "Don't let that slide"
- "You can't handle this"

But this is where what you learned earlier applies:

Your voice has to be the loudest.

In the Middle of a Trigger, Tell Yourself

- "I don't have to react right now."
- "I can handle this differently."
- "This feeling will pass."

You Are Your Own Support in That Moment

You are not waiting for someone else to calm you down.

You are learning how to do it yourself.

Skill: STOP Method

S	— **Stop**	—	Pause. Don't react immediately.
T	— **Take a Breath**	—	Slow your body down.
O	— **Observe**	—	• What am I thinking? • What am I feeling? • What is happening around me?
P	— **Proceed**	—	Choose your next step carefully.

Worksheet: My Triggers

Things that trigger me:

____

____

____

____

What I usually think in those moments:

____

____

____

____

What I usually do:

____

____

____

____

Worksheet:
My New Response Plan

When I feel triggered, I will:

1. ____

2. ____

3. ____

A statement I will tell myself:

____

____

____

____

One healthier response I can try:

____

____

____

____

Worksheet:
Urge Tracking

What triggered the urge:

How strong was the urge (1–10):

What I did instead:

What happened after:

Journaling Page

- What triggers me the most?

- What helps me slow down?

- What gets in the way of responding differently?

CLOSING THOUGHT

You are not trying to control everything.

You are learning how to respond differently one moment at a time.

And that is how change happens.

Pillar III

Alignment: Living in Integrity

Alignment means making choices that support the life you are building. In this pillar, you will learn how to regulate emotions, grow through hard moments, and face cravings without giving in.

07 Emotional Regulation: Managing Your Emotions Without Letting Them Manage You

Emotions are not the problem.

But the way we respond to them can be.

What Emotional Regulation Really Means

Let's define this clearly.

Emotional regulation is about managing your emotions, not allowing them to manage you.

That does not mean:

- Ignoring your feelings
- Suppressing them
- Pretending they don't exist

It means:

- Understanding what you feel
- Allowing it to be there
- Choosing how you respond

Why This Matters

For many people, substance use became a way to:

- Escape emotions
- Control emotions
- Avoid emotions

Because emotions can feel:

- Overwhelming
- Unpredictable
- Intense

The Pattern

Emotion $\rightarrow$ Discomfort $\rightarrow$ Reaction

And the reaction often becomes:

- Using
- Avoiding
- Shutting down
- Exploding

The Shift

Emotion $\rightarrow$ Awareness $\rightarrow$ Choice

You Are Not Your Emotions

You experience emotions.

But you are not controlled by them—unless you allow them to take over.

Emotions Are Signals

Every emotion is telling you something.

- Anxiety $\rightarrow$ "Something feels uncertain or unsafe."

- Anger $\rightarrow$ "Something feels wrong or crossed a boundary."

- Sadness $\rightarrow$ "Something matters and feels lost or heavy."

The Goal Is Not to Get Rid of Emotions

The goal is:

To understand them—and respond intentionally.

Anxiety: When Your System Is Activated

Anxiety is one of the most common emotional experiences.

And one of the most misunderstood.

What Anxiety Actually Is

Anxiety is your body preparing for something.

Even if nothing is actually happening.

What It Feels Like

- Racing thoughts
- Urgency
- Tight chest
- Difficulty sitting still
- Restlessness

Important Truth

You cannot think your way out of anxiety.

You have to calm your body first.

What Helps

- Slow breathing
- Movement
- Grounding
- Connection

Medication and Anxiety

For some people, anxiety is not just situational.

It is ongoing.

And in those cases:

Medication can help stabilize your system so you can actually use your skills.

This is not about weakness.

It is about support.

The Role of Medication in Emotional Stability

Let's be direct.

If your system is constantly unstable:

- Emotional regulation becomes harder
- Triggers feel stronger
- Impulses increase

Medication Can Help With:

- Mood stabilization
- Thought clarity
- Anxiety reduction
- Emotional balance

But Medication Is Not the Whole Solution

It supports you.

It does not replace:

- **Skills**
- **Awareness**
- **Growth**

Consistency Matters

Inconsistent use leads to:

- Emotional instability
- Increased symptoms
- Higher relapse risk

Key Truth

Stability supports emotional regulation.w

Emotional regulation supports change

Connection: You Are Not Meant to Regulate Alone

Emotional regulation is not just internal.

It is also relational.

We Regulate Through Connection

Being around safe people helps:

- **Calm your system**   • **Reduce intensity**   • **Bring clarity**

This Connects Back to Your Village

The right people:

- Help you stay grounded
- Help you think clearly
- Help you regulate

Isolation Increases Emotional Intensity

When you are alone with your thoughts:

- Emotions can feel bigger
- Thoughts can spiral
- Urges can increase

Connection Brings Balance

Even a simple connection helps:

- **Talking**   • **Sitting with someone**   • **Being around safe people**

Grounding and Centering Yourself

Grounding brings you back to the present.

Centering brings you back to yourself.

Grounding (External Awareness)	Centering (Internal Awareness)
• What do I see?	• What am I feeling?
• What do I hear?	• What do I need right now?
• Where am I right now?	• What matters in this moment?

Spiritual Component: Returning to Yourself

This is where the deeper work happens.

Not religion.

But connection.

Spirituality in Emotional Regulation

Spirituality here means:

- Being connected to yourself
- Being aware of your inner state
- Acting in alignment with your values

When You Are Centered

You are:

- Less reactive
- More intentional
- More grounded

Simple Centering Statement

"I don't have to react right now. I can choose."

The Power of Waiting

This is one of the most important skills you can learn.

Waiting Is Not Doing Nothing

Let's be clear.

Waiting is not avoidance.

Waiting is:

Gathering information before making a decision.

When You Don't Wait

You:

- React emotionally
- Act impulsively
- Make decisions you later regret

When You Wait

You:

- Observe
- Understand
- Think
- Choose intentionally

Waiting Creates Space

Between:

- Feeling
- And action

Example

Emotion: Anger

Without Waiting

Immediate reaction

→ Words said

→ Situation escalates

With Waiting

Pause
Observe
Breathe
Think

→ Choose response

This Is Emotional Strength

Not reacting immediately.

Emotional Growth: Becoming Stronger, Not Just Getting Through

For a long time, you may have learned to just "get through" things.

Push through.

Hold it in.

Deal with it later.

But that's not the goal here.

This is not about tolerance. This is about growth.

Let's Be Clear About the Difference

Tolerance says:	Growth says:
• "Just get through it"	• "Understand it"
• "Hold on until it passes"	• "Learn from it"
	• "Become stronger through it"

This Is Not Just About Resilience

Resilience is often talked about as:

- "Bouncing back"
- "Getting through hard things"

But we're going deeper than that.

This is about becoming stronger, more aware, and more capable over time.

You Are Not Just Surviving Emotions

You are learning to:

- Understand them
- Respond to them
- Work with them
- Grow through them

What Emotional Growth Looks Like

Over time, you begin to notice:

- You pause more before reacting
- You understand what you're feeling
- You don't act on every impulse
- You make more intentional decisions

Growth Takes Practice

At first, it will feel like:

- Slowing down is uncomfortable
- Sitting with emotions is difficult
- Waiting feels unnatural

That's because it's new.

But Over Time

You build:

- **Awareness**
- **Control**
- **Confidence**

This Is Strength

Not:

- **Avoiding emotions**
- **Escaping discomfort**

But:

Being able to stay present, understand what's happening, and respond intentionally.

Sitting With Your Emotions — Learning Instead of Escaping

This is where most people struggle.

What It Means to Sit with Emotions

It means:

- Allowing the feeling to be there
- Not escaping it
- Not immediately reacting

But This Is Not Just About Sitting

This is about:

Learning from what you feel.

When You Sit With an Emotion, Ask:

- What is this feeling trying to tell me?
- What triggered this?
- What do I need right now?

This Turns Emotion Into Information

Instead of something you:

- Fight
- Avoid
- Escape

It becomes something you:

- Learn from
- Understand
- Use

What You Build Over Time

- Emotional awareness
- Better decision-making
- Less impulsive behavior
- Stronger sense of control

Real-Life Example

Situation

You feel anxious and overwhelmed.

Old Pattern

Use
Avoid
Escape

New Pattern

Pause
Breathe
Ground
Wait
Understand

→   Choose a healthier response

What Changes Over Time

You don't just "get through" the moment.

You come out of it with:

- More awareness
- More control
- More confidence

This Is the Work

Not avoiding emotions.

Not being controlled by them.

But:

Learning how to experience them, understand them, and grow through them.

Worksheet: Understanding My Emotions

What emotion do I struggle with most:

____

____

____

What does it feel like in my body:

____

____

____

What do I usually do when I feel this:

____

____

____

Worksheet:
My Waiting Plan

When I feel overwhelmed, I will:

1. ____

2. ____

3. ____

What I will remind myself:

____

____

____

____

Worksheet:
Grounding and Centering

What helps me feel grounded:

____

____

____

____

What helps me feel centered:

____

____

____

____

Who I can connect with:

____

____

____

____

Journaling Page

- What emotions do I try to avoid?

- What happens when I sit with them instead?

- What am I learning about myself?

CLOSING THOUGHT

You don't have to get rid of your emotions.

You just have to learn how to handle them.

You are not here to be controlled by how you feel.

You are here to understand it, respond to it, and grow stronger because of it.

08 Emotional Growth in Hard Moments: What to Do When Things Feel Like Too Much

There will be moments when everything feels like too much.

Not just uncomfortable.

Not just stressful.

But overwhelming.

You may feel like:

- "I can't handle this."
- "I need something right now."
- "This feeling isn't going to stop."

These are the moments that matter most.

Because these are the moments where:

Old patterns try to take over.

This Chapter Is About Those Moments

Not when things are calm.

Not when you're thinking clearly.

But when:

- Emotions are high
- Your body is activated
- Your mind is moving fast

Let's Be Clear

You will have hard moments.

Becoming healthy does not remove them.

What changes is:

How you move through them.

When It Feels Like Too Much

In those moments, your system is overloaded.

- Your thoughts speed up
- Your emotions intensify
- Your body reacts

You Are Not Thinking Clearly in That Moment

That's not a flaw.

That's how the brain works under stress.

So the Goal Is Not to "Figure Everything Out"

The goal is:

Get through the moment without making it worse.

Step One: Recognize What's Happening

Say to yourself:

"This is one of those moments."

That alone creates awareness.

Step Two: Stabilize First, Not Solve

This is where people get stuck.

They try to:

- Solve the problem
- Fix everything
- Make a big decision

While overwhelmed.

That Usually Leads to:

- Impulsive decisions
- Regret
- Escalation

Instead

Focus on:

Stabilizing your body and mind first.

Step Three: Ground and Center

You already learned this—but now we apply it under pressure.

Grounding (External)

- Look around
- Name what you see
- Feel your feet on the ground

Centering (Internal)

- What am I feeling right now?
- What do I need right now?

Simple Statement

"I don't have to act right now."

Step Four: Reduce the Intensity

You are not trying to eliminate the feeling.

You are trying to:

Bring it down enough to think clearly.

Ways to Lower Intensity

- Slow breathing
- Splash cold water
- Step outside
- Sit still and focus on your body
- Call someone

This Is Not Avoidance

This is regulation.

The Urge Wave (Revisited)

In these moments, urges can feel strong.

What It Feels Like

- "I need something right now"
- "I can't sit with this"
- "This is too much"

What's Actually Happening

Your brain is looking for relief.

Fast.

But Remember

Urges come in waves.

They:

- Rise
- Peak
- Fall

Your Job

Ride the wave.

Not act on it.

The Power of Waiting (In Real Time)

This is where everything you learned in Chapter 7 applies.

Waiting in Hard Moments

Waiting is not:

- Doing nothing
- Ignoring the situation

Waiting is:

Giving yourself time to gather information before acting.

In These Moments, Tell Yourself

- "I don't have to decide right now."
- "I can wait 10 minutes."
- "I can come back to this."

Why This Works

Because intensity decreases over time.

Your Voice Matters Most—Especially Here

When you're overwhelmed, other voices get loud:

- "Just do it."
- "You can't handle this."
- "This will make it better."

But this is where you use what you built:

Your voice has to be the loudest.

Say to Yourself

- "I've been here before. I can get through it."
- "This feeling will pass."
- "I don't have to go backwards."

This Is You Showing Up for Yourself

Not perfectly.

But intentionally.

Growth Happens in These Moments

Not when things are easy.

But when they are hard.

This Is Where You Build Strength

Every time you:

- Pause instead of react
- Wait instead of act impulsively
- Choose differently

You are reinforcing:

A new pattern.

Real-Life Example

Situation

You feel overwhelmed, anxious, and triggered.

Old Pattern

Use
Avoid
Escape

New Pattern

Recognize
Pause
Ground
Wait
Reach out

$\rightarrow$ Move through the moment

What Changes Over Time

You begin to notice:

- The intensity feels more manageable
- You don't react as quickly
- You trust yourself more

Emergency Plan (Have This Ready)

When things feel too intense, don't try to figure it out in the moment.

Have a plan.

My Plan When Things Feel Like Too Much

1. ____

2. ____

3. ____

People I Can Reach Out To

1. ____

2. ____

3. ____

Things I Can Do Instead of Using

- ____

- ____

- ____

Worksheet:
My Hard Moments

What situations overwhelm me most:

____

____

____

What I feel in those moments:

____

____

____

What I usually do:

____

____

____

What I will try next time:

____

____

____

Journaling Page

- What happens when I feel overwhelmed?

- What makes it harder?

- What helps even a little?

____

____

____

____

____

____

____

____

CLOSING THOUGHT

You don't need to control everything.

You don't need to feel perfect.

You just need to:

Get through the moment without going backwards.

And every time you do that, you are building a life you can stay in.

Cravings and Urges: Understanding Them Without Giving In

Cravings are one of the most misunderstood parts of addiction.

They can feel:

- Strong
- Immediate
- Overpowering

And in those moments, it can feel like:

"I don't have a choice."

Let's Be Clear

You do have a choice.

But in the moment, it may not feel like it.

What Is a Craving?

A craving is:

A strong desire or urge to use a substance.

But it's more than just a thought.

It involves:

- **Your mind**   • **Your body**   • **Your emotions**

Cravings vs. Urges — What's the Difference?

People often use the words "craving" and "urge" as if they mean the same thing.

They're related, but they're not the same.

Understanding the difference helps you respond more effectively.

What Is an Urge?

An urge is:

A sudden pull or impulse to do something.

It usually shows up quickly.

What Urges Feel Like

- Immediate
- Intense
- Action-driven
- "I need to do this right now"

Urges are often:

- Short-lived
- Triggered by a moment
- Strong, but brief

Example of an Urge

You feel stressed.

Your mind says:

"Do it right now."

That's an urge.

What Is a Craving?

A craving is:

A deeper, more sustained desire for a substance or behavior.

It builds over time and can last longer.

What Cravings Feel Like

- Lingering
- Mental and emotional
- Repetitive
- Hard to ignore

Cravings often involve:

- Thoughts ("I need this")
- Feelings (stress, emptiness)
- Physical sensations

Example of a Craving

You've been thinking about using for hours.

It keeps coming back.

It feels like:

"I really want this."

Key Difference

Urge	Craving
• Quick	• Builds over time
• Intense	• Lasts longer
• Short-lived	• Mental + emotional
• Action-focused	• Repetitive

Why This Matters

Because how you respond can be different.

How to Handle an Urge

Urges require:

Immediate pause and interruption.

What Helps

- STOP method
- Delaying action
- Grounding
- Changing your environment

And Most Important—Replace the Action

If you don't replace the behavior, your system will keep pushing you back to it.

Instead of acting on the urge:

- Move your body
- Drink water
- Step outside
- Shift your environment immediately

How to Handle a Craving

Cravings require:

Ongoing awareness and replacement.

What Helps

- Understanding the trigger
- Staying connected
- Replacing the behavior
- Re-centering on your goals

Replacement Is Essential Here

Cravings are stronger when there is a void.

If you remove the substance but don't replace it:

- Your mind keeps going back
- The craving stays active
- The pattern continues

Both Require the Same Core Skills

- Awareness
- Waiting
- Grounding
- Choosing your response
- **Replacing the behavior**

Important Truth

Neither urges nor cravings last forever.

Even if they feel like they will.

You Don't Have to Fight Them

You don't have to:

- Force them away
- Panic
- Act immediately

You can:

- Notice them
- Understand them
- Move through them

And Replace Them

This is where change actually happens.

Cravings Are Not Just Physical

People often think cravings are only physical.

But they are also:

- Emotional
- Mental
- Environmental

Cravings Are Learned

Your brain has learned:

"This = relief"

So when something feels uncomfortable...

Your brain automatically goes back to what worked before.

This Is Not Weakness

This is conditioning.

And conditioning can be changed.

How It Changes

Not just by stopping.

But by:

Replacing the old pattern with a new one.

The Craving Cycle

Trigger $\rightarrow$ **Thought** $\rightarrow$ **Urge** $\rightarrow$ **Action** $\rightarrow$ **Relief**

The relief is what reinforces the cycle.

Even if it's temporary.

Breaking the Cycle

You don't break it at the end.

You break it in the middle.

Between urge and action.

And You Replace the Action

That is what creates a new pattern.

The Urge Wave (Going Deeper)

Cravings and urges feel like they will last forever.

But they don't.

They Move Like Waves

They:

- Rise
- Peak
- Fall

Most Don't Last Forever

They often:

- Peak within minutes
- Decrease if you don't act on them

Your Job

Ride the wave—not react to it.

And Replace While You Ride It

You don't just sit there.

You choose something else.

What Makes Cravings Stronger

- Being alone
- Being in familiar environments
- Emotional stress
- Fatigue
- Hunger
- Boredom

This Is Why Structure Matters

Your environment and routine influence your cravings.

Spiritual Component: Who You Are Becoming in This Moment

This is one of the most important parts of this chapter.

Because cravings are not just physical or mental.

They are also:

Moments of identity.

In the Middle of a Craving, You Are Choosing

Not just behavior.

But direction.

Ask Yourself

- "Who am I becoming right now?"
- "What direction does this choice take me?"

Spirituality Here Means Alignment

Not religion.

But alignment with:

- **Your values**
- **Your purpose**
- **The life you are building**

Cravings Pull You Back

They pull you toward:

- **Old habits**
- **Old identity**
- **Old patterns**

Spiritual Grounding Pulls You Forward

It reminds you:

- Who you are becoming
- What you are building
- Why you started

Short Centering Statement

"This moment matters."

"This choice matters."

"I'm choosing who I'm becoming."

Meaning Replaces Impulse

Instead of asking:

"How do I get rid of this feeling?"

Ask:

"What does this moment require from me?"

This Is Spiritual Strength

Not avoiding the moment.

But being present in it—with intention.

Your Voice Matters Here Too

Cravings and urges come with strong internal voices:

- "Just do it"
- "You need this"
- "You can't handle this without it"

But Remember

Your voice has to be the loudest.

Say to Yourself

- "I don't have to act on this"
- "This is an urge—it will pass"
- "This is a craving—I can move through it"
- "This is not who I'm becoming"

Real-Life Example

Situation

You feel stressed after a long day.

Old Pattern

Thought: "I need something to relax"

→ Use

New Pattern

Thought: "I'm stressed, but I can handle this differently"

→ Pause
→ Ground
→ Wait
→ Replace
→ Re-center

Replacement Is the Turning Point

Let's be clear:

You cannot just remove a behavior—you have to replace it.

If You Don't Replace It

- The craving stays active
- The mind keeps searching
- The old behavior returns

If You Do Replace It

- You interrupt the pattern
- You build a new response
- You strengthen control

Replacement Can Be Physical, Emotional, or Spiritual

Physical Replacement	Emotional Replacement	Spiritual Replacement
Walk	Talk to someone	Reflect on your purpose

• Move	• Journal	• Reconnect to your values
• Drink water	• Sit with the feeling	• Remind yourself who you are becoming

Connection Helps Reduce Cravings

Cravings grow in isolation.

Connection Is Also a Spiritual Practice

Because it reminds you:

- You are not alone
- You are supported
- You are part of something bigger

Connection Replaces Isolation

And that changes everything.

Emergency Craving Plan

When a craving or urge hits, I will:

1. ____

2. ____

3. ____

People I can reach out to:

1. ____

2. ____

3. ____

Healthy replacements I will use:

____

____

____

Spiritual reminders I will use:

____

____

Worksheet: Understanding My Cravings and Urges

What usually triggers my cravings or urges:

____

____

____

____

What I feel in my body:

____

____

____

____

What I think in those moments:

____

____

____

____

Is this usually a quick urge or a longer craving?

____

____

____

____

What I actually need instead:

____

____

____

____

What I will replace it with:

____

____

____

____

Journaling Page

- What do cravings teach me about myself?

- What helps me stay grounded in those moments?

- Who am I becoming when I choose differently?

CLOSING THOUGHT

Cravings and urges are part of the process.

But they are also moments of choice.

You are not just avoiding something.

You are building something.

And every time you pause, wait, and replace, you become stronger, more aware, and more aligned with the life you are creating.

Pillar IV

Connection — Your Village

Healing does not happen in isolation. In this pillar, you will explore grounding, support, healthy relationships, and the importance of choosing the right people.

10 Anxiety and Calming Your System: Practical Tools and Guided Meditation

Anxiety is one of the most common experiences when doing something new.

And one of the most misunderstood.

You may feel like:

- Your mind won't slow down
- Your body is always on edge
- You can't relax, even when nothing is happening
- Something bad is about to happen—even if you don't know what

Let's Be Clear About Anxiety

Anxiety is not just "overthinking."

Anxiety is your body and mind preparing for something, whether it's real or not.

Why Anxiety Feels So Strong

Because it's not just mental.

It's physical.

What Happens in Your Body

- Your heart rate increases
- Your breathing becomes shallow

- Your muscles tighten
- Your thoughts speed up

Important Truth

You cannot think your way out of anxiety.

You have to calm your body first.

The Anxiety Cycle

Trigger → Thought → Body Reaction → More Thoughts → More Anxiety

Example:

"I feel off" → "Something is wrong" → Body tightens → "This is bad" → Anxiety increases

Breaking the Cycle

You don't start with your thoughts.

You start with your body.

Calming Your System (Step-by-Step)

Step 1: Slow Your Breathing

Simple Breathing Practice

- Inhale slowly for 4 seconds
- Hold for 2–3 seconds
- Exhale slowly for 6 seconds

Repeat for a few minutes.

Why This Works

It tells your body:

"You are not in danger right now."

Step 2: Ground Yourself

Bring yourself back to the present.

5–4–3–2–1 Method

- 5 things you see
- 4 things you feel
- 3 things you hear
- 2 things you smell
- 1 thing you taste

This interrupts the anxiety loop.

Step 3: Center Yourself

Grounding brings you to the present.

Centering brings you back to yourself.

Ask:

- What am I feeling right now?
- What do I need right now?

Simple Centering Statement

"I am here. I am okay. I can get through this."

The Spiritual Component: Calming Beyond the Mind

Anxiety often disconnects you from yourself.

It pulls you into:

- Fear
- Future thinking
- Uncertainty

Spiritual Grounding Brings You Back

Not to a belief system.

But to:

- Presence
- Awareness
- Connection

Spirituality in Anxiety Management Means

- Being present in the moment
- Trusting that you can handle what comes
- Staying connected to your values and direction

When Anxiety Rises, Ask Yourself

- "What is actually happening right now?"
- "Am I safe in this moment?"

Spiritual Reset Statement

"I am grounded. I am present. I am not in danger."

Medication and Anxiety

Let's be honest.

Sometimes anxiety is not just situational.

It is ongoing.

When That Happens

Your system may need support.

Medication Can Help With

- Reducing baseline anxiety
- Stabilizing your nervous system
- Making it easier to use your coping skills

This Is Not a Weakness

It is a tool.

Important Reminder

Medication works best when it is:

- Taken consistently
- Combined with skills
- Part of a larger plan

Connection Helps Calm Anxiety

Anxiety grows in isolation.

When You Are Alone	When You Connect
• Thoughts spiral	• Your body calms
• Fear increases	• Your thoughts slow
• Your system stays activated	• You feel more grounded

Connection Is Also a Spiritual Practice

Because it reminds you:

- You are not alone
- You are supported
- You are part of something bigger than this moment

The Power of Stillness

When anxiety hits, your instinct is to:

- **Move**   • **Escape**   • **Fix something**

But sometimes, the most powerful thing you can do is:

Be still.

Stillness Is Not Doing Nothing

It is:

Choosing not to react immediately.

In Stillness, You Can

- Observe what's happening

- Feel without reacting
- Allow your system to settle

Guided Meditation: Calming Anxiety in the Moment

Sit comfortably.

Feet on the ground.

Hands relaxed.

Close your eyes if you feel comfortable.

Take a slow breath in...

...and slowly breathe out.

Again...

Inhale slowly...

Exhale slowly...

Now bring your attention to your body.

Notice:

- Your feet
- Your legs
- Your hands
- Your breathing

Say quietly to yourself:

"I am here."

"I am safe right now."

If your thoughts start to race, that's okay.

Do not fight them.

Just bring your attention back to your breath.

Inhale...

Exhale...

Now bring your focus to the present moment.

Not the past.

Not the future.

Just right now.

Say to yourself:

"This feeling will pass."

"I can handle this moment."

Take one more slow breath in...

...and out.

When you're ready, slowly open your eyes.

Guided Meditation: Grounding and Centering

Sit or stand comfortably.

Take a deep breath in...

...and slowly release it.

Bring your awareness to where you are.

Look around.

Notice your surroundings.

Now bring your focus inward.

Ask yourself:

- What am I feeling right now?

No judgment.

Just awareness.

Now place your hand on your chest or stomach.

Feel your breath.

Say:

"I am connected to myself."

"I am grounded."

"I can move through this."

Stay here for a few moments.

Then slowly return your attention to the room.

Worksheet:
My Anxiety Patterns

What triggers my anxiety:

____

____

____

What I feel in my body:

____

____

____

What I usually think:

____

____

____

What helps calm me:

____

____

____

Worksheet:
My Calm Plan

When I feel anxious, I will:

1. ____

2. ____

3. ____

What I will tell myself:

____

____

____

____

Who I can reach out to:

____

____

____

____

Journaling Page

- When does my anxiety show up most?

- What helps me feel grounded?

- What do I need more of in my life to feel calm?

CLOSING THOUGHT

Anxiety does not mean something is wrong with you.

It means your system is activated.

You don't have to fight it.

You don't have to escape it.

You can:

Calm your body, center yourself, and move through it.

And every time you do, you build more control, more awareness, and more peace.

11 Building Healthy Relationships and Your Village

This is not meant to be done alone.

That doesn't mean you can't do the work yourself.

But long-term sobriety is not just about what you do individually.

It is also about:

Who you surround yourself with.

Let's Be Clear About This

A healthy village is essential to securing and maintaining sobriety.

Not optional.

Not extra.

Essential.

Because the people around you will either:

- Support your growth
- Or pull you back into old patterns

Why Your Village Matters

Your environment influences:

- Your thinking
- Your decisions
- Your behavior
- Your identity

If You Are Around People Who:

- Normalize substance use
- Avoid growth
- Live in chaos
- Disrespect boundaries

Then over time:

That becomes your normal.

If You Are Around People Who:

- Support your sobriety
- Respect your boundaries
- Encourage your growth
- Live with intention

Then over time:

That becomes your direction.

What Is a Village?

Your village is:

The group of people you allow to influence your life.

But it's more than just people around you.

Your village is made up of people you love—and just as important, people who genuinely love you.

These are people who:

- Care about your well-being
- Support your growth
- Encourage you to do better
- Respect your direction

Your Village Is Also Your Support System

These are the people:

- You can call when you feel overwhelmed
- You can reach out to when you feel yourself slipping back into old patterns
- Who will be honest with you
- Who will help keep you on track

A Real Village Does Not Enable You

They don't:	They:
Ignore your behavior	Speak truth
Encourage unhealthy patterns	Support your growth
Stay silent when you're going in the wrong direction	Help you stay aligned with your goals

Your Village Holds You Up When You Feel Weak

When you're struggling:

- They remind you who you are
- They remind you what you're building
- They help you stay grounded

This Is What Makes a Village Different

Not just presence.

Not just history.

But:

Support, accountability, care, and alignment with your growth.

Family vs. Relatives

This is important.

Because many people confuse the two.

Relatives

Relatives are:

People you are connected to by blood or legal relationship.

Family

Family is:

People who support you, respect you, and contribute to your growth.

Important Truth

Just because someone is your relative does not mean they are your family.

And:

Just because you do not share DNA does not mean someone cannot be your family.

Defining Family: What It Really Means

For many people, the word *family* is confusing.

Because it is often used to describe people you are related to.

But, it's important to understand:

Family and relatives are not the same thing.

Relatives Are Based on Biology

Relatives are:

People you are connected to by blood, marriage, or legal relationship.

You don't choose your relatives.

Family Is Based on Relationship

Family is:

People who consistently show up for you in a healthy, supportive way.

A True Family Member Is Someone Who:

- Supports your growth
- Respects your boundaries
- Encourages your sobriety
- Is honest with you
- Wants to see you do well
- Shows care through their actions—not just words

Important Truth

Not everyone you are related to is safe for you.

And:

Not everyone who loves you knows how to support you in a healthy way.

Another Important Truth

Just because someone is your relative does not mean they have earned a place in your village.

Family Is Built on How People Show Up

Not:

- What they say
- What they promise
- What they used to be

But:

How they consistently show up in your life right now.

You Are Allowed to Redefine Family

This is one of the hardest parts of building your new life.

Because it may require you to:

- Create distance from certain relatives
- Set boundaries with people you've always been close to
- Accept that some relationships are not healthy

But You Are Also Allowed to Expand Family

Family can include:

- Friends
- Mentors
- People you meet on your treatment journey
- Support systems

Key Principle

Family is not about DNA. It is about alignment, support, and consistency.

Ask Yourself

- Does this person support my sobriety?
- Do I feel stable around them?
- Can I be honest with them?
- Do they respect my boundaries?

If the Answer Is No

Then they may be a relative.

But not part of your family in this season of your life.

This Is Not About Disrespect

This is about:

Protecting your growth.

You Can Care About Someone Without Giving Them Access

You can:

- Love someone
- Respect someone
- Care about someone

And still:

Not allow them to influence your sobriety.

Closing Thought on Family

You don't choose who you're related to.

But you do choose:

Who you call family.

And in on this journey:

That choice matters.

The Role of Your Village

Your village helps you:

- Stay accountable
- Stay grounded
- Stay connected
- Stay focused

When You Struggle

Your village:

- Helps you think clearly
- Reminds you of your goals
- Supports you through difficult moments

Without a Healthy Village

- Isolation increases
- Old patterns return
- Triggers become stronger
- Relapse risk increases

You Have to Define
What "Healthy" Means for You

This is where the work becomes personal.

Ask Yourself

"What kind of people do I need around me to support my growth and my sobriety?"

A Healthy Person for You Might Be Someone Who:

- Respects your sobriety
- Does not pressure you to use

- Supports your boundaries
- Communicates honestly
- Lives with some level of stability
- Is working on themselves

You Have to Be Honest Here

Not based on:

- History
- Loyalty
- Obligation

But based on:

What actually supports your sobriety.

Red Flags That Can Lead to Relapse

Some relationships increase your risk.

Even if you don't want to admit it.

Red Flags Include:

- Encouraging or minimizing substance use
- Disrespecting your boundaries
- Creating drama or chaos
- Being inconsistent or unreliable
- Making you feel guilty for changing
- Not supporting your growth

Important Truth

You cannot build a healthy life in an unhealthy environment.

Boundaries: Protecting Your Growth

Boundaries are not about controlling others.

They are about:

Protecting yourself.

A Boundary Sounds Like:

- "I'm not going to be around that."
- "I can't do that anymore."
- "This is what I need right now."

You Don't Need Permission to Set Boundaries

And not everyone will like them.

That's okay.

Boundaries Are Part of a Healthy Life

Without them:

- Old patterns return
- People cross lines
- You lose stability

Spiritual Component: Alignment and Energy

This goes deeper than behavior.

Your Village Affects Your Energy

The people around you influence:

- How you feel
- How you think
- How you show up

Spiritual Awareness in Relationships Means

- Being aware of how people affect you
- Not ignoring what you feel around others
- Choosing alignment over familiarity

Ask Yourself

- "Do I feel stable around this person?"
- "Do I feel supported or drained?"
- "Do I feel like I can grow around them?"

This Is About Alignment

Not comfort.

Not history.

Not obligation.

Alignment with the life you are building.

You Will Outgrow Some People

This is part of sobriety.

Growth Changes Your Environment

As you grow:

- Your priorities change
- Your behaviors change
- Your mindset changes

And Not Everyone Will Grow with You

That does not make you wrong.

It means:

You are moving forward.

This Is Not About Cutting Everyone Off

It's about being intentional.

Some Relationships May Need:

- Distance
- Boundaries
- Limits

Others May Become Stronger

When they:

- Support your growth
- Respect your direction

Building Your Village Intentionally

You don't just "end up" with the right people.

You build your village.

Places to Find Healthy Connections

- Treatment programs
- Support groups
- Sober communities
- Mentorship
- Structured environments

Look for People Who Are:

- Consistent
- Honest
- Accountable
- Growth-oriented

You Also Have a Role in Your Village

It's not just about what you receive.

It's also about what you bring.

Ask Yourself

- Am I showing up honestly?
- Am I respecting others?
- Am I growing?

Healthy Relationships Go Both Ways

Worksheet: Defining My Village

Who is currently in my life:

____

____

____

Who supports my growth:

____

____

____

Who may not be healthy for me right now:

____

____

____

What "healthy" means for me:

____

____

Worksheet: My Boundaries

Boundaries I need to set:

____

____

____

____

Where I need more distance:

____

____

____

Where I feel most supported:

____

____

____

Worksheet: Building My Village

People I want to bring into my life:

____

____

____

Qualities I am looking for:

____

____

____

Steps I can take to build connection:

____

____

____

Journaling Page

- What relationships support my sobiety?

- What relationships make it harder?

- What kind of village do I want to build?

CLOSING THOUGHT

You don't just recover by changing your behavior.

You recover by changing your environment.

The people around you matter.
The love around you matters.
The village you build matters.

And when you build it intentionally, you give yourself a real chance at lasting sobriety.

12 Romantic Relationships and Dating, Protecting Your Sobriety While Building Connection

Romantic relationships can be powerful.

They can bring:

- Connection
- Meaning
- Support
- Growth

But they can also bring:

- Emotional instability
- Distraction
- Triggers
- Relapse risk

Let's Be Direct

Romantic relationships can either support your sobriety or derail it.

Why This Matters

When you are on your journey, you are:

- Rebuilding your life
- Learning emotional regulation
- Developing new patterns
- Strengthening your identity

A Relationship Can Impact All of That

Positively or negatively.

The Risk of Replacing One Dependency with Another

One of the most common patterns on this journey is:

Replacing substance use with a relationship.

Instead of:

- Using a substance to cope

You begin:

- Using a person to regulate your emotions

What This Looks Like

- Constantly needing contact
- Feeling unstable when they are not available
- Losing focus on your sobriety
- Making decisions based on the relationship, not your growth

Important Truth

A relationship cannot replace your work.

A Relationship Should Complement, Not Complete You

This is one of the most important things to understand.

Because many people enter relationships believing:

- "I need someone to feel whole."
- "This person will fix how I feel."
- "I won't feel this way if I'm with someone."

Let's Be Clear

A relationship is not there to complete you. It is there to complement you.

You Are Already Whole

You are:

- Complete
- Capable
- Enough

With or without a relationship.

A Relationship Should Add, Not Replace

A healthy relationship:

- Adds value to your life
- Supports your growth
- Enhances what you are already building

It Should Not:

- Fill a void
- Replace your identity
- Become your source of stability

If It Does, It Becomes a Risk

Because anything you depend on to feel okay can also destabilize you when it changes.

The Cake and the Icing

Think of it like this:

You are the cake.

The relationship is the icing.

The cake stands on its own.

It is already:

- Whole
- Complete
- Solid

The icing:

- Adds to it
- Enhances it
- Makes it better

But the cake does not depend on the icing to exist.

If You Build Your Life Like This

You don't lose yourself in relationships.

You don't depend on them for stability.

You choose them intentionally.

Value Matters

Anyone you allow into your life should:

Bring value and not take it away.

Ask Yourself

- Does this person add to my life or drain it?
- Do I feel stronger or weaker around them?
- Am I growing or becoming unstable?

Important Truth

If a relationship is taking more from you than it is giving, it is not supporting your sobriety.

Timing Matters

Not every relationship is bad.

But timing is important.

The Early Stage of Your Sobriety Is a Vulnerable Time

You are:

- Emotionally adjusting
- Learning new skills
- Becoming more aware

A Relationship Too Early Can:

- Distract you
- Overwhelm you
- Pull you into old patterns

Ask Yourself

- Am I stable right now?
- Am I grounded?
- Can I maintain my progress without losing myself in this relationship?

What Makes a Relationship Healthy

A healthy relationship should:

- Support your sobriety
- Respect your boundaries

- Encourage your growth
- Not create chaos

A Healthy Partner:

- Does not pressure you to use
- Respects your sobriety
- Communicates openly
- Is emotionally stable
- Is accountable for their behavior

A Healthy Relationship Feels Like:

- Calm, not chaotic
- Supportive, not draining
- Stable, not unpredictable

Red Flags in Romantic Relationships

These are serious.

Because they can lead directly to relapse.

Red Flags Include:

- Substance use or encouraging use
- Emotional instability
- Manipulation or control
- Disrespect for your boundaries
- Constant conflict or drama
- Making you feel guilty for prioritizing your sobriety

Important Truth

You cannot build a healthy relationship on an unstable foundation.

Emotional Triggers in Relationships

Relationships can activate:

- Abandonment fears
- Emotional reactivity
- Trust issues
- Trauma responses

This Is Especially Important With:

- Trauma history
- Depression
- Anxiety
- Mood instability

What Happens If You're Not Aware

- You react instead of respond
- You become emotionally overwhelmed
- You lose focus on your sobriety

Spiritual Component: Relationships and Alignment

This goes deeper than attraction.

Not Every Connection Is Meant for You

Just because:

- You feel something
- There is chemistry
- There is history

Does not mean:

It is aligned with your growth.

Spiritual Awareness in Dating Means Asking:

- "Does this person support who I am becoming?"
- "Do I feel grounded or unstable around them?"
- "Does this relationship move me forward or backward?"

Connection vs. Alignment

You can feel connected to someone...

And still not be aligned with them.

Alignment Is What Matters

Maintaining Yourself in a Relationship

You cannot lose yourself in a relationship.

You Still Need To:

- Maintain your routines
- Attend treatment/support
- Use your skills
- Stay connected to your village

Important Truth

A relationship should be part of your life—not your entire life.

Boundaries in Romantic Relationships

Boundaries are essential.

Examples of Healthy Boundaries

- "I'm not going to be around substance use."
- "My sobriety comes first."
- "I need time for myself and my growth."

If Someone Cannot Respect Your Boundaries

They are not healthy for you.

You Are Responsible for Your Sobriety

Not your partner.

Not the relationship.

You.

A Relationship Can Support You

But it cannot carry you.

Real-Life Example

Situation

You start dating someone who drinks regularly.

Old Pattern

Ignore it
Adapt to it
Eventually get pulled back into use

New Pattern

Recognize the risk
Set boundaries
Make a decision based on your sobriety

Healthy Dating Guidelines

- Take your time
- Don't rush emotional attachment
- Stay aware of your triggers
- Keep your sobriety first
- Pay attention to behavior, not just words

Worksheet:
Relationship Check-In

How does this person affect me emotionally:

____

____

____

Do I feel stable or unstable around them:

____

____

____

Do they support my sobriety:

____

____

____

Are there any red flags:

____

____

Worksheet:
My Boundaries in Relationships

What I will not accept:

____

____

____

____

What I need in a relationship:

____

____

____

____

What I will protect no matter what:

____

____

____

____

Journaling Page

- What does a healthy relationship look like for me?

- What patterns do I need to avoid?

- Am I choosing connection or alignment?

____

____

____

____

____

____

____

____

____

Relationships can be powerful.

CLOSING THOUGHT

But they should not cost you your sobriety.

You are already whole.
You are the foundation.

And the right person will:

Add to your life, not define it.

Pillar V

Purpose — Moving Forward

Your new life is not just about what you stop. It is about what you build. In this pillar, you will protect your growth, define your purpose, and strengthen long-term sobriety.

13 Boundaries in Action: How to Protect Your Sobriety in Real Life

Boundaries are one of the most important tools you have.

But knowing what boundaries are...

And actually using them...

Are two very different things.

Let's Be Clear

Boundaries are not optional; they are necessary.

Because without boundaries:

- People cross lines
- Old patterns return
- You lose stability
- Relapse risk increases

What a Boundary Actually Is

A boundary is:

A clear limit you set to protect your well-being, your sobriety, and your growth.

It is not about controlling other people.

It is about:

Controlling what you allow into your life.

Boundaries Answer One Question

"What is okay for me—and what is not?"

Why Boundaries Are Hard

Let's be honest.

Boundaries are not easy.

Common Reasons People Struggle

- Fear of hurting others
- Fear of rejection
- Guilt
- Wanting to keep the peace
- Not being used to putting themselves first

Important Truth

Just because something is uncomfortable does not mean it is wrong.

Boundaries Protect You

Your sobriety requires:

- Stability
- Structure
- Safety

Without Boundaries

You allow:

- Chaos

- Pressure
- Triggers

With Boundaries

You create:

- **Clarity**   • **Protection**   • **Consistency**

Types of Boundaries You Need

1. Environmental Boundaries

These protect where you go and what you are around.

Examples

- Not going to places where substances are present
- Leaving situations that feel unsafe
- Choosing people who support your growth

2. Relationship Boundaries

These protect who you allow into your life.

Examples

- Limiting time with people who jeopardize your sobriety
- Not engaging in toxic dynamics
- Choosing people who support your growth

3. Emotional Boundaries

These protect your mental and emotional space.

Examples

- Not taking on other people's emotions
- Not engaging in arguments that escalate
- Stepping away when overwhelmed

4. Time and Energy Boundaries

These protect how you use your time.

Examples

- Prioritizing healthy activities
- Saying no to things that drain you
- Making time for rest and self-care

What Boundaries Sound Like

Boundaries are clear and direct.

They do not need long explanations.

Examples

- "I'm not going to be around that."
- "That doesn't work for me."
- "I can't do that right now."
- "I need to step away."

You Do Not Need Everyone to Agree

This is important.

Because when you set boundaries:

- Some people will not like it
- Some people will push back
- Some people will test it

Important Truth

Someone else being uncomfortable does not mean your boundary is wrong.

How People Respond to Your Boundaries Tells You a Lot

Healthy people:

- Respect your boundaries
- Adjust their behavior
- Support your growth

Unhealthy people:

- Ignore your boundaries
- Push against them
- Try to make you feel guilty

Pay Attention to That

It tells you who belongs in your village.

Boundaries and Guilt

You may feel guilty when you set boundaries.

That Does Not Mean You Are Doing Something Wrong

It means:

- You are doing something new
- You are breaking old patterns

You Can Feel Guilty—and Still Set the Boundary

Boundaries Require Consistency

A boundary is not what you say once.

It is what you consistently enforce.

If You Set a Boundary but Don't Follow Through

People learn:

- They don't have to respect it

Consistency Builds Respect

Real-Life Examples

Situation 1: Someone Offers You a Substance

Boundary	Action
"I'm not doing that anymore."	You leave if needed.

Situation 2: Someone Creates Drama

Boundary	Action
"I'm not getting into this."	You disengage.

Situation 3: Someone Disrespects You

Boundary	Action
"This is important to me. I'm not going to compromise it."	You create distance if necessary.

Spiritual Component: Boundaries as Self-Respect

Boundaries are not just behavioral.

They are also spiritual.

Setting Boundaries Means

- You recognize your worth
- You honor your growth
- You respect your direction

Spiritual Alignment in Boundaries

You choose:

- What aligns with your life
- What supports your purpose
- What strengthens your identity

Ask Yourself

- "Does this situation align with who I am becoming?"
- "Is this protecting or harming my growth?"

Boundaries Keep You Aligned

They help you stay:

- Grounded

- Focused
- Intentional

You Are Allowed to Change

As you grow:

- Your boundaries may change
- Your tolerance for certain behaviors may decrease

That Is Not a Problem

That is growth.

You Can Care Without Allowing Access

This is one of the most important things to understand.

You can:

- Love someone
- Care about someone
- Respect someone

And still:

Not allow them into your space.

This Is Not About Being Harsh

It is about being:

- Clear
- Honest
- Protective of your new life

Worksheet:
My Boundaries

What I need to protect in my life:

____

____

____

____

Situations where I need stronger boundaries:

____

____

____

____

People I need boundaries with:

____

____

____

____

Worksheet: Boundary Statements

A boundary I need to set:

____

____

____

____

How I will say it:

____

____

____

____

How I will follow through:

____

____

____

____

Worksheet: Boundary Reflection

What makes boundaries hard for me:

____

____

____

____

What I am afraid will happen:

____

____

____

____

What I know I need anyway:

____

____

____

____

Journaling Page

- Where do I struggle to set boundaries?

- What happens when I don't?

- What would change if I started protecting myself more?

____

____

____

____

____

____

____

____

____

Boundaries are not about pushing people away.

CLOSING THOUGHT

They are about:

Protecting what matters.

And in your new life:

Your growth, your stability, and your sobriety matter.

You are allowed to protect that.

Identity, Purpose, and Building a Life You Can Stay In

At some point in recovery, the focus shifts.

It's no longer just about:

- Not using
- Avoiding relapse
- Getting through the day

It becomes about something deeper.

Who are you becoming?

Because long-term sobriety is not sustained by avoidance.

It is sustained by:

Building a life that you actually want to live.

Your Life Is Not Just About What You Stop

It's about what you build.

You are not just:

- Removing substances
- Breaking old patterns

You are:

- Rebuilding your identity

- Creating direction
- Establishing purpose

Identity: Who You Believe You Are

Your identity shapes everything.

- Your decisions
- Your relationships
- Your behavior
- Your future

Old Identity vs. New Identity

Old Identity May Sound Like:

- "This is just who I am"
- "I've always been like this"
- "I can't change"

New Identity Sounds Like:

- "I'm learning who I am"
- "I'm building something different"
- "I'm becoming more stable, more aware, more intentional"

Important Truth

You are not defined by your past.

You are shaped by what you do moving forward.

You Are Rebuilding Yourself

This is not about going back to who you were.

It is about:

Becoming someone new.

That Requires

- Awareness
- Consistency
- Intentional decisions

You Cannot Be All Versions of Yourself at Once

There is something important to understand about growth.

Three versions of you will never exist in the same space at the same time:

- Who you were
- Who you are
- Who you are becoming

You Are Always Moving Between These States

You are not stuck.
You are not fixed.

You are:

Constantly changing and evolving.

But Growth Is Not Automatic

Just because time passes does not mean growth happens.

You Have a Choice in Who You Become

It is up to you to determine who you are and what you will become.

You are not just drifting through life.

You are making decisions every day that shape:

- Your identity
- Your direction
- Your future

Ownership Matters

This is where responsibility comes in.

Not in a negative way.

In an empowering way.

You have to take ownership of your life.

Because at the end of the day:

You are the one who has to live with the outcomes of your choices.

That Includes:

- The decisions you make
- The people you allow into your life
- The patterns you continue or change
- The direction you choose

This Is Not About Blame

It's about control.

When You Take Ownership

You gain:

- Power
- Direction
- Clarity

When You Don't

You feel:

- Stuck
- Reactive
- Controlled by circumstances

Spiritual Component: Identity Beyond the Past

This is where the work becomes deeper.

Spirituality here is not about religion.

It is about:

- Meaning
- Connection
- Identity
- Direction

Spiritual Identity Means

You are not just:

- Your mistakes
- Your past behavior
- Your lowest moments

You are:

Someone who is growing, evolving, and becoming.

Becoming With Intention

Spiritual growth means:

Being intentional about who you are becoming.

Ask Yourself

- "Am I living like the person I want to become?"
- "Do my actions reflect my future or my past?"

You Exist in the Middle

You are not your past self.
You are not yet your future self.

You exist in the space between.

And:

What you do in that space determines everything.

Daily Decisions Shape Identity

Every time you:

- Pause instead of reacting
- Set a boundary
- Choose growth
- Stay aligned

You move closer to:

The person you are becoming.

Purpose: Why You Keep Going

At some point, you need more than:

- "I don't want to relapse."

You need:

A reason to stay.

Purpose Does Not Have to Be Big

It doesn't have to be:

- Perfect
- Fully figured out

It can be:

- Taking care of yourself
- Being present
- Building stability
- Showing up consistently

Purpose Gives Direction

Without direction:

- You drift
- You fall back into old patterns

With direction:

You move forward even when it's difficult.

Connection to Something Greater Than the Moment

When things get hard, you need something to hold onto.

That Can Be:

- Your values
- Your direction
- Your purpose
- Your growth

Spiritual Grounding Statement

"I am not who I used to be. I am becoming who I am meant to be."

Building a Life You Can Stay In

This is the goal.

Not just:

- Getting clean
- Staying sober

But:

Creating a life you don't want to escape from.

What That Life Includes

- Stability
- Healthy relationships

- Purpose
- Structure
- Meaning

Structure Creates Stability

You need:

- **Routine**   • **Consistency**   • **Direction**

Without Structure	With Structure
• You drift	• You stay grounded
• You become reactive	• You stay focused
• Old patterns return	• You stay stable

Daily Life Matters

Change is not just about big moments.

It is built in:

- Daily habits
- Small decisions
- Consistent effort

Ask Yourself

- What does my day look like?
- Does it support my sobriety?

Spiritual Alignment in Daily Living

This is where spirituality becomes practical.

It is not just what you believe.

It is:

How you live.

Alignment Means

Your actions match:

- Your values
- Your goals
- Your direction

When You Are Aligned

You feel:

- More grounded
- More clear
- More stable

When You Are Not Aligned

You feel:

- Disconnected
- Unstable
- Pulled in different directions

Your Life Should Reflect Your Growth

Not your past.

That Means

- Choosing environments carefully
- Choosing relationships intentionally
- Making decisions that support your future

You Are Responsible for Your Life Now

This is important.

Not in a blaming way.

But in an empowering way.

You Are Responsible For:

- **Your decisions**
- **Your direction**
- **Your growth**

This Is Where Everything Comes Together

- Your thoughts
- Your emotions
- Your relationships
- Your boundaries
- Your habits

All of it builds your life.

Real-Life Example

Old Pattern	New Pattern
Wake up without direction	Wake up with structure
React to the day	Stay connected
Avoid discomfort	Use skills
Use	Make intentional decisions → Build stability

Worksheet: My Identity

Who I used to believe I was:

____

____

____

____

Who I am becoming:

____

____

____

____

What I want my identity to be:

____

____

____

____

Worksheet: My Purpose

What matters to me:

____

____

____

____

What I am working toward:

____

____

____

Why I want to stay in my sobriety:

____

____

____

Worksheet: My Life Structure

What my daily routine looks like:

____

____

____

____

What supports my stability:

____

____

____

What I need to improve:

____

____

____

Journaling Page

- What kind of life do I want to build?

- What does that look like day-to-day?

- What steps am I taking toward that life?

CLOSING THOUGHT

Sobriety is not just about avoiding something.

It is about becoming someone.

You are not stuck.

You are not defined by your past.

You are:

Building a life, building yourself, and shaping who you will become.

And that work is what keeps you moving forward.

15 Long-Term Sobriety: Maintaining Growth and Preventing Relapse

This is not a moment.

It is not a phase.

It is not something you complete.

Your sobriety is something you maintain.

Because the truth is:

You don't just "arrive" at a place where nothing affects you anymore.

Let's Be Clear

Relapse is not random.

It is usually the result of:

- Small decisions
- Unaddressed emotions
- Disconnection
- Loss of structure

Over time.

Understanding Relapse Before It Happens

Relapse does not start with using.

It starts earlier.

The Three Stages of Relapse

1. Emotional Relapse

You are not thinking about using yet.

But your behavior changes.

Signs

- Isolating
- Avoiding support
- Not expressing emotions
- Increased stress
- Poor self-care

2. Mental Relapse

Now your mind begins to shift.

Signs

- Thinking about using
- Romanticizing past use
- Minimizing consequences
- Internal conflict ("I shouldn't... but I want to")

3. Physical Relapse

This is the action.

- Using again

Important Truth

By the time you get to physical relapse, the process has already been building.

Prevention Starts Early

You don't wait until things are out of control.

You pay attention early.

Ask Yourself Regularly

- Am I isolating?
- Am I staying connected?
- Am I taking care of myself?
- Am I being honest with myself?

The Role of Structure in the Long-Term

Structure is what keeps you grounded.

Without Structure	With Structure
You drift	You stay focused
You become reactive	You stay stable
Old habits return	You stay aligned

Structure Includes

- Routine
- Sleep
- Nutrition
- Movement
- Support systems

Connection Is Not Optional

You cannot maintain sobriety in isolation.

When You Disconnect	When You Stay Connected
• Your thoughts get louder	• You stay grounded
• Your emotions intensify	• You get feedback
• Your perspective narrows	• You stay accountable

Spiritual Component: Staying Connected to Your Why

Over time, it's easy to forget:

- Why you started
- What you've built
- What matters

Spiritual Maintenance Means

- Staying connected to your purpose
- Staying aware of your direction
- Staying aligned with your values

Ask Yourself Regularly

- "Why does this matter to me?"
- "What am I building?"
- "Who am I becoming?"

Spiritual Grounding Statement

"I've come too far to go back."

Triggers Don't Go Away Your Response Changes

You will still experience:

- **Stress**
- **Emotional pain**
- **Difficult situations**

The Difference Is

You now have:

- Awareness
- Skills
- Support
- Choice

Complacency Is a Risk

This is important.

Complacency Sounds Like

- "I'm good now"
- "I don't need to do all that anymore"
- "One time won't hurt"

Complacency Leads To

- Less structure
- Less connection
- Less awareness

And eventually:

Increased risk.

Growth Must Continue

Sobriety is not just about maintaining.

It is also about continuing to grow.

Ask Yourself

- What am I working on now?
- Where am I growing?
- What needs attention in my life?

Your Village Still Matters

Everything you learned earlier still applies.

Your Village Helps You Stay on Track

They:

- Notice changes
- Offer support
- Help you stay accountable

You Will Have Difficult Moments

Even in long-term sobriety.

The Goal Is Not to Avoid Difficulty

The goal is:

To respond differently when it happens.

Have a Plan Before You Need It

Don't wait until you are overwhelmed.

Know Ahead of Time

- Who you will call
- What you will do
- How you will respond

Relapse Prevention Plan

Warning Signs I Need to Watch For

____

____

____

____

What I Will Do If I Notice Them

____

____

____

____

Who I Will Reach Out To

____

____

____

____

Returning to Basics

When things feel off:

Go back to what works.

- Structure
- Grounding
- Connection
- Boundaries

Spiritual Alignment

This is where everything comes together.

Long-Term Stability Comes from Alignment

Your:

- **Actions**
- **Relationships**
- **Decisions**

All need to match:

The life you are building.

When You Stay Aligned

You feel:

- **Grounded**
- **Clear**
- **Stable**

When You Don't

You feel:

- **Disconnected**
- **Unsettled**
- **At risk**

You Are Still Responsible

This does not change.

You Are Responsible For

- Maintaining your growth
- Staying aware
- Making intentional decisions

Real-Life Example

Early Warning Signs
Isolating
Skipping routines
Feeling overwhelmed

Old Pattern

Ignore it
Avoid it
Use

New Pattern

Recognize
Reach out
Re-engage
Stabilize

→ Stay on track

Worksheet:
My Warning Signs

Signs I may be slipping:

____

____

____

____

What I will do when I notice them:

____

____

____

____

Worksheet:
My Support Plan

People I can reach out to:

____

____

____

____

What helps me stay grounded:

____

____

____

____

Worksheet:
Staying Aligned

What matters most to me:

What I am building:

What keeps me on track:

# Journaling Page

- What helps me stay consistent?

- What puts me at risk?

- What do I need to stay focused long-term?

CLOSING THOUGHT

Your new life is not about perfection.

It is about consistency.

You don't have to get everything right.

You just have to stay aware, stay connected, and keep moving forward.

And every day you do that, you protect the life you've worked to build.

www.ingramcontent.com/pod-product-compliance
Lightning Source LLC
Chambersburg PA
CBHW081925120726
47997CB00010B/3040